CLOSE CASKETS

May these words Reach your heart

Donté Clark

BY

DONTÉ CLARK

SELECTED POETRY

PACIFIC RAVEN PRESS, LLC

A Pacific Raven Original

Close Caskets is published by
Pacific Raven Press, LLC
P.O. Box 678
Ka`a`awa, HI 96730

Email: pacificravenpress@yahoo.com
Business Telephone: 808-228-1630
Fax: 808-237-8974
pacificravenpress.co

Selected & Edited by Karla Brundage

FIRST EDITION

ISBN 978 0 9993039 8 6

Book design & production by Fred Dodsworth
Contact: fdodsworth@comcast.net
fleurdumalpress.com

Front cover illustration: Monica Rose M @brushed_by_rose
Back cover photograph: Donté Clark by Dorean Raye photography

Printed by BR Printing in San Jose, California

–

Foreword by Dr. Khalid White

2020 was a year that began with so much promise, hope, and optimism. 2020 was the beginning of a new decade, one replete with "2020 Vision." Suddenly that all took a drastic turn and 2020 became the deadliest year in U.S. history. The year 2020 literally became a matter of life and death. A year of *close caskets*.

According to the Center for Disease Control (CDC), America suffered more than 3 million deaths in 2020. More than 3 million caskets. There was no shortage of causes of death in 2020. Americans experienced a perfect storm of causes: political turmoil, wildfires, hurricanes, economic depression, racial violence, opioid addiction, and, of course, the Coronavirus.

There is a cultural colloquialism that states, *When White America catches a cold, Black America catches pneumonia.* That sentiment held true as Black America suffered from an ungodly "pneumonia" the entire year of 2020. The sickness's symptoms included disproportionate coronavirus deaths, an increased health gap, and an ever-increasing wealth gap.

What's more is this deadly sickness began showing itself in ways Black America never imagined. A tragic loss of global luminary the Black Mamba, Kobe Bryant. An untimely demise of cultural hero the Black Panther, Chadwick Boseman. Black America lost legendary, civil rights leaders C.T. Vivian and John Lewis, too. Even more, the traumatic murders of unarmed Black citizens George Floyd, Breonna Taylor, and Ahmad Arberry occurred. 2020 brought Black America some very, very close caskets.

One thing about Black America, however, is that our artists depict our collective feelings and experiences. If you listen closely enough our artists offer social solutions. For example, when Sam Cooke said, *A Change Is Gonna Come*, when Marvin Gaye asked, *What's Going On?* and Aretha Franklin advised the world to, *Think about what you're trying to do to me*, there were social justice messages couched within those songs. Artist/author, Donté Clark, carries on in that tradition.

Donté's second book of poems, *Close Caskets*, provides readers a contemporary view into the lived experiences of many of Black America's youth and young adults. From the eyes of chocolate-hued boys and girls *Born Pissed* growing up in America's inner cities, to the emotions of transitional aged youth that are in harm's way by simply waiting at the *Bus Stop*, to the the inner thoughts of a hungry youngster that could give you *33 Reasons* why he won't remain hungry all day.

Donté Clark paints vivid poems about Troublesome young men, with names like *Rodney*, *JJ*, and *Chuk*. Young men that may not get to celebrate reaching the milestones of their *21st*, *25th* or their *30 Peace*. These poems tell the stories of young people in Richmond, CA, a city of pride and purpose where caskets remain ever so close to Black lives.

Donté's book provides a snapshot of Black life. A combination of social justice, harsh realities, coupled with optimism for better conditions in the future. The book delivers the substance that we have longed for after experiencing such a highly troubling year.

Just to think, this perfect storm of unprecedented losses in 2020 birthed a global movement for Black lives, created an enormous voter turnout in the latest elections and helped usher in a new political regime that will include the first Black female Vice President. If 2020 brought the caskets closer to Black America, then 2021 brings a sense of hopefulness even closer.

Black America should be encouraged by these accomplishments, and Black America should be encouraged by Donté Clark. Encouraged by his brilliance, resilience, and his greatness. Encouraged that he has chosen to use his pen to shine even brighter after all the darkness that engulfed so many of us in 2020. He represents us.

Complete darkness enables the stars to shine even brighter. And in the book, *Close Caskets*, our young brother uses the year 2021 to shine brighter than he has ever shined.

Acknowledgements

First, foremost, and above all I'd like to acknowledge and thank my Heavenly Father, my creator, for being enormously merciful and gracious towards me. There were times in my life that seemed unbearable; death showed his teeth and I walked through unscathed. You deserve all the glory, Abba. To my earthy parents, Donald and Sophia, thank you for raising me to be thoughtful and considerate of others, and for pouring all that you had to give into my siblings and I. Thank you to my Grandparents for the stories and big personalities that shaped my childhood, for every ancestor that came before us who I'd like to learn more about.

To all of my siblings, Lisa, Keisha, Donald, DeAnzer, Derrick, Nyiesha, Donisha, and Shawny. I love you all and all of your children. To my love and life partner, Boopie, thank you for being a genuine soul. Thank you to all of my aunties and uncles, my cousins by blood or by struggle, I enjoyed every moment we spent together. Let's make more memories before it's over.

Thank you to all of Richmond, CA, especially the neighborhoods I grew up in, Parchester Village, North "Narf" Richmond, Central, and Southside. Each person I met along the way, who has ever offered me some game or encouragement, I thank you.

Thank you to the Making Waves Educational Program for literally saving my life. There are too many people to name, but all of you know exactly who you are. Thank you for the field trips, college tours and providing me with the biggest opportunity, too. Both opportunities saved my life.

Shout out to the Ryse Center members who have been my partners in justice for ten years. We've made history together! With all of me, I am super humbled and grateful for my Raw Talent family. Y'all are my hearts. o Molly Raynor, my sister, we did it! We did everything we said we'd do. Thank you for every show, poem, retreat, parking lot hanging three hours after work, and for touring the world with me. We'll never forget what we've done and continue to do!

Shout out to my real ones at Youth Speaks for looking out for me and providing me a platform to grow. Only the real ones though!

Thank you to my *Romeo is Bleeding* crew, family, for filming my life and showing the world our Richmond story. Y'all have become family, and I thank you. Don't always agree with your haircuts, but I thank you nonetheless.

And a great big thank you to Pacific Raven Press, all the work and support from Karla Brundage and Tyrice Brown for helping me turn these pages into something beautiful out of the tragedy. Thank you!

Also, shout out to my Ypsilanti, Ann Arbor family. Y'all are like another Raw Talent for me, so I love y'all! Thank you to Kenny Kahn, for your love and support as big bro. Brother Deen for your wisdom and game, Ms Linda for being like an ainty and partner in the courtroom, Dr. Marshall and Malcolm Marshall for your support and encouragement, Khalid White for being a counselor and big bro. To Chinaka Hodge, for years and years of support, love and being and inspiration, Briana Swain for being solid and a great support and friend, Brandon Santiago for being my soul brother, for always encouraging and being a beautiful person. Thank you Amber Butts for being willing to assist me in my writing. Thank you Anisa, Philippa Kelley, and Luis Rodriguez for reading the book and giving your thoughtful reflections and praise for the book! Thank you! And anyone else I may have not mentioned here, charge it to my mind not my heart!

Special shoutouts: To every high school that I have ever had an opportunity to speak to or perform for. For every Instagram like, comment, subscription, DM, and repost that I've received. To every juvenile detention center that I've visited and those who have written me letters, To all my folks in San Quentin. My heart is for you.

Shoutout *The North Pole Show* family. Another classic time in my life. Thank you to everyone who supported or participated on that project.

Thank you to anyone that I have ever hurt or misled on my pathway to know freedom. Please know that I sincerely apologize. Thank you to those who have forgiven me. To all of the people who were lost to the streets, who have ever made eye contact with me, a head nod or a gesture of endearment, I love you, and not a day goes by without me thinking of you.

To every courtroom attorney who has ever invited me into the fight for their client's justice, for their piece of freedom. It's on forever. To all of the teachers who taught me the best they knew how.

To all the writers out there speaking your story and bringing truth to power. I see you and I'm inspired. To all of my favorite writers (I'll name y'all another time) but I am watching and studying you. I see you.

Lastly, to whomever you are that wishes harm upon me, I forgive you. I'm out here too, see you when I see you, slick.

All praise to the Most High!! Selah.

Donté Clark

Donté Clark previously published: *Know Freedom* (CreateSpace Independent Publishing Platform. October 2018). Available on Amazon.

Note to Readers:

The idea of *Close Caskets* is to remind, challenge and encourage all ears to un-busy themselves and to seek silence, in order to hear our true selves speak. It is a reminder to press forward to the voice in the wilderness, crying out in a desolate place beckoning for all eyes to reflect on our journey from as far back as to the now, and to question, how did we get here? Where are we? Who are we? Where are we headed?

Pause. Acknowledge. Be an active participant in the grieving and renewal process and see oneself as a reflection of one people. Who I am is how I treat you. *Close Caskets* is about looking back, looking within, and pouring out all of the broken pieces, embracing what remains and pressing forward. We have to *Close Caskets* to one day *Knowfreedom*.

Donté

TABLE OF CONTENTS

TABLE OF CONTENTS

QUIET STORM

BONES REBIRTH

LEAD POISONIN'

B-4 Becomin'

bein' born blak
      bearin' blues by brothas buried
      beneath bridges

burned bodies belittled before becomin'
better. beyond broken but believin'

because brotherhood builds
      beautiful bonds

bypassin' bullies brute billy bats
beatin'
blacks
back-bone
breakin'

burdened by balancin' books   bullets bricks

barren blocks blown by bombs

billowin' blues billy blew back before bus boy-cotton
brung benefits. be barely breathin'

between blitz brought by babylonians
baphomets biopics be blackberries

bent below bulky branches bruh.

There Was an Explosion of Lead

that erupted his body
to blood memory

all of his life cut down to seconds

of booms

smokey air 'nd shriekin' tires
twirl through stop lights
as the engine cuts corners
leavin' a drunk night to plop its weight
on the silence

before a concert of sirens

the body's gold teeth stained with a currant drip

spillin' cries for mama out
of his left cheek into the ears of the
concrete

a red coat over the petals of young flowers
stemmin' through...

to be watered by blood.

Orgy

they orgasm
when they kill us

show me a news clip
with our face down

our ass up
with legs spread opened 'nd wet

twitchin' 'nd moanin'
with our eyes rollin' back as we take it

'nd there you'll see, on the screen
seduced by the ears

that you are an addict consumer
of media porn

the orgy of buck rearin'

when these white folks
reach in their pants 'nd pull out their loaded pipes

on camera, with the world watchin' american streets
the whites be like

fucking niggers

yea fuck these niggers

'nd they mean it too

to see us lion in the street
'nd their aim is to kill the pussy.

Pray For

for the blocks, the streets, the corners
that drip at the head from the lives of men
that pours down the sideburns like hot oil on a coarse scalp

for the neighborhoods that sit between the legs
of a tired city
harsh spoken 'nd brash with heavy hands
combin' swiftly
through thick waves of african roots
forcibly brushin' out the indigenous kinks 'nd cookabugs
nappin' 'nd curled in the back of the mind familiar
like moms 'nd pop's kitchen. pray

for concrete   for the cracks that blister dry
like chapped lips 'nd
teeth sharp as bullets that chew down skin
gnawin' its beauty of black to raw pink.

pray for friday nights that gather the shots
'nd have not been proven to be bulletproof
when the night rises our sons fall. pray for moons

who slither slim to full again ministerin' at twilight
praised holy by congregation of mourners
howlin' from the hollow streets 'nd front porch pews
in the wee hours of service between the cyclin'
of blunt offerin's 'nd hennessy tithes

who can count the sinner's hands that are a loud clap
of amens, shouts, 'nd stomps when loved on, feel their spirit
talkin' in tongues from touch of racist bullets.

Born Pissed

without a pot to piss in

raised down poverty street over
make you opposition

losin' common sense
to bottomless pockets

picketin' picket fence probably
won't profit poor people.

will it?

not in america.

chocolate children smilin' cavities
duck duck goose chasin' underground railroads to safe
havens or heaven.

where white man's dreams
fall from 4th of july sky

all while we still catchin' hell

hell.

just a freeway exit away

flow straight 'nd blow right through the light

'nd brake two lefts 'nd to the right you
be there.

hell

you'll see hella people
hella high hopin' like hell to spread wings

above telephone wires 'nd shoe strings

pass shoeless jimmy 'nem
puffy eyed leanin' back
to a time worth dreaming bout

a helluva winter
these 60 years
been

still ain't figured
if where i'm at is hella hot or cold as hell

hell. all i know is
these bullets burn

'nd it's some cold muthafuckers shootin' 'nem.

DONTÉ CLARK

Butterfly Rests On A Gator's Brow

seekin' peace while ridin'
the beast

tears i speak for da' homeless child

soul of a man burst throughout streets

world's gotta jonez fa'rotten my bones

must be my wayfarin' passin' through

cry, beggin' moan, still,
left alone

lost, ain't knowin' much to do

some days i'm sittin' sittin' sittin' cause i'm feeble 'nd in need
i've seen no difference my affliction to a grave they carry me

i'm fed off bread of tears.

Bare Arms

i don't care if you bare arms
the size 'nd strength of bears' arms
if you ain't got the heavenly power
to tower over you
when they bear arms then yo' sad
sad mama 'nd all
the widows 'nd windows
on her dilapidated street
gon' have to eye-ball yo beautiful body
shake 'nd leak out
all of her motherly dreams
for you in her bare arms
ya damn fool.

DONTÉ CLARK

Bus Stop

waitin' at the bus stop
where the boy was shot
22 times is regular.

every passin' car poses a threat
u-turns bother my skin 'nd
slow drivers turn my stomach.

damn man,
this bus is hella late. it's cold out here
'nd i'm just tryin' to get to the crib.

the bus is probably 'bout to bend this corner in a minute. watch.

wait,
hold up. why…is this car drivin' so slow.
is it stoppin'?

shiid, fuck that bus.

2nd Period

there were math problems not taught to me in second period.
a marathon of numbers that had me slump postured twistin' dreads
    in back of the class
with some ill equations flashin' beneath my yankee fitted thinkin' cap.

like if mom's bills cost 2 birthdays 'nd a christmas
'nd all i have is 2 wooden nickels but i'm 2 prayers short
how much hunger do i need for the sum to cover the difference

2 pistols plus a 30 clip= y?

y not?

y i gotta wake up
530 'nd walk 8 blocks for a bus stop
pay a dolla somethin' out of the 6 mama scraped me
ride 45 mins up the street to sit 8 hours in 6 classes
pledge allegiance to a bloody flag, count they math
science they lab, date they past, on a 10 month drag
'nd i still ain't passed...

all chip bags come half empty.
but crumbs from the blue strips be finger lickin temptin'.

is 5 years of ballin' worth 25 'nd an elbow?

how much hunger do i need for the sum to cover the difference?

33 Reasons

under the sunrise
is poverty

under poverty is
a ceilin'

under a ceilin'
is a hoody

beneath the hoody
is a boy

beneath the boy
is hunger

on the side of the hoody
on the boy with hunger
is a barrel

beneath the barrel
is 33 reasons why he won't be hungry for long.

Gimme

so you
tryna tell
me that
all of 4
hunnid
yeeaas
ain't
pose to
be a
razor
slit on'a
tip of
my lips
with a
trigger
finga
itch in
my
twitch
with a
pimp hand
land'n hard
on a bih
big toe
steppin
outside
reppin'
wit a
twist
diamond
cut
necklace
on'a jit
slit slit.

leave
ya neckless
for da
strip
blitz
bliss
drippin'
on'a
trip
black
rage
buckin'
on'a
skit
granny
prayed
mama
prayed
cuffs
off
my
wrist
all
section
8
hate
raised
not a
cent
done
beggin'

cracka
for a
crumb
or the
pick
finna
fitna
fitna
fitna
start
takin'
mo'
risks
snatch
'nd
grab
get
the bag
from'da
rich

jack move
jack move
jack. move.
gimme
this

gimme gimme gimme gimme gimme.

There Is Blood

between
us

where climbin' fences
'nd throwin' rocks
meant good
times

when splashin' water
meant swimmin'
'nd all nighters
was sleep
overs

when we were only
pretendin' to
be cops
'nd

robbers were more
fittin' than the
clothes our
mothers
bought
us

when our lips made bullet sounds
'nd our fingers were pistols
with water balloons burstin'
instead of blood
tissue

when our hide 'nd seeks carried sugar'd
laughs 'nd harmless tags of touch
'nd reachin' home base
meant that you
were safe

before street signs
'nd corner stores
claimed
us

before high schools
'nd hats renamed
us

before county jails
'nd rollin' hills
spaced
us

there is blood between us.

2/3rd Shootin' Stars

hard headed with cold shoulders
stiff necks 'nd stout hearts
tongues that tear through those   tender
why won't we wake?

eyes a blood stream of christ offerin'
deep pit of me redlined a food desert
helpless hands held high hopes. how
2/3rds will face   the lake

happy feet that leap to close caskets
a flock of street brides widowed bastards
night skin fall on cameras

shootin' stars shows such sadness
shootin' stars shows such sadness
shootin' stars shows such sadness
shootin' stars shows such sadness

2/3rds doomed to such fate.

Close Caskets

cuz crack cocaine causes
colored cities crimson currents

contributing cyclical coma counts
compilin'
corner-store candlelights

close caskets. capturin'
choice choirs carryin' cathedrals

cuz constant casualties crush
colored community's cheer. cold.
cold *cold*.

CASKET PRETTY

all of my niggas are casket pretty — noname

7th Seal

doom
stands over
the black waters
feignin' its
yellow teeth.

its body
hail fire
mingled
with
blood
drippin'
over a third
lot of
the land.

searin' herb
'nd tree at
the root.

'nd the
waters
are troubled
with the
peaked blast
of trumpets.

as strong wind
slaps soot
across
the cheek
of sun 'nd
moon.

spillin' stars

into the
black deep
turnin' its
waves bitter.

as doom
leans
over the waters
swoopin'
down its
fury
to no end
the waves
will cry out
for
death, but
death will flee
from its shores.

My 18th

it's like being
a newborn baby for
the 18th time.

it's my eyes openin'
to tears in a twin bed 'nd
forcin' my body to the carpet

pockets hurtin', with no new nothin'
to be fresh to death in.

it's the shock
the weight
the break.

it's the
taste of
thanksgivin'
on mornin' breath
'nd the fact that there is
breath to be thankful for
in mournin.'

it's not foreseein'
the day of your
birth another year
past 15 but it's
present.

it's tears
of joy
'nd
survivor's
guilt.

it's flippin' pages
in your memory
two months back
to December 07
to the mornin' of the bullet
'nd death of mista boo
he was 20. 'nd young.
killed before 21.

it's pullin' back the bedsheet
that covers your window sill
open to skylight
'nd inhale the day. it's the sun
starin' into your soul
sayin' *welcome.*

as your mind flips
back two more pages
to september 07
day 11th
to the bullet
'nd death of d-red.
he, 21. 'nd young.
buried 2 weeks later…
'nd many others coffined for his blood.

it's feelin'
like
birthdays be the worst days
cause most ain't make another year 'nd that shit
hurts mayne.

'nd it's
also bein' cool
enough to enjoy
this pain for another year.

you know, for da ones who ain't here. hear?

Duboce (pronounced as Du-boyz)

i remember the nights of shivers endured in the black hoody

the common posturin' of backbone 'nd a raised foot
against the fadin' paint of green-store entrance 'nd metal gate

the fullness of our ears to the chatter
in a cypher of our lips to the blunt

with all eyes red low 'nd on guard to the turnin' wheels of the street

whether bank roll sloppy or (k)not

we always could feel the world's hand in our pockets

jump man dreamin' to be fly at 23
profits from scores of the rock made us cornerstones of duboce

DONTÉ CLARK

600 Banks Drive

childhood at 600 banks drive was no curfew

it was made bed, 'nd house chores done
before fixin' yo lips to ask mama 'bout some outside.

'nd anywhere further than front porch 'nd sidewalk
mama's ears better have heard of it before.

any new places could only be gone to with old faces
cause mama ain't like us playin' with no new names.

she wanted to know where we was goin'
'nd with who we said we was goin' with

you better be where you say you be
'nd call home if you gon be longer than you know to.

don't make me come lookin for you, hear me? 'cause wherever
you show yo ass, that's where i'm gonna hand it to you.

back then, a bunch of head nods 'nd
ok mama, we will got us out the door fast.

it was my older brother derrick, my younger sister shawny
'nd i that grew up in this house. mama set the rules, 'nd daddy paid the bills.

our childhood was everythin' to love
cause 600 banks drive was no curfew.

it was outside all day before the street lights shined loud enough to notice

'nd at least one of us kept an eye up to the sky

had to make sure night ain't set in over the footprints of the sun too long before we all went back to check home.

ya gotta let mama see that ain't none of yo bones broke,
ain't no drugs in ya, 'nd ain't none of ya teeth missin'.

ya better smell like ya been playin' outside too 'nd nothin' else.

cause mama didn't want us bein' too fast. just children.

everyday dinner would be almost ready 'bout time of the street lights

'nd mama made it clear, if we was gon' come in to eat after our play
we better had stayed in cause ain't no in 'nd out of mama's house after dark.

we made sure to wash our hands before we ever went into the kitchen
'nd we didn't eat anythin' from mama's kitchen in front of our outside company
that we ain't plan on sharin'.   cause mama didn't like that.

but it wasn't many times that we came in to eat unless we was stayin' inside

cause as crackin' as our block was, we wanted every bit of night hours we can grab

because 600 banks drive was no curfew

'nd the sun seemed to stay out longer for us.

or maybe our days stretched further because
our sunrise was a bike ride race up 'nd down the street

with scrawny legs pedalin' wheelies on 10 speeds

zoomin' flash with no helmets

shirtless

or shirts flappin' from our backs like parachutes
'nd our mouths wide open to the clouds

sometimes we made ramps out of milk crates 'nd wood boards

laid them right there on top of speed bumps for a dare to fly

'nd if we fall 'nd scraped our smooth we'd get right up. a lil scratch of
  blood don't hurt.

as more kids came outside
we began to crowd the front yards with the softest grass 'nd royal rumbled

the biggest person usually got jumped, 'nd the smallest person was thrown
  every which way

grown ups ain't like us horse playin' as we did.
so whenever they saw one too many choke holds
'nd groups of us stompin' each other, some elder
would peak out their curtain
or front door 'd give us an ear full 'bout
breakin' somethin'
on somebody
'nd hurtin' ourselves,
so we'd stop.

'cause 600 banks drive was a love thy neighbor type of street.
wasn't a face on the whole block that was unfamiliar.

all us kids rotated yards up 'nd down the street as we played

we kicked balls over fences 'nd climbed over to get them

played pinky or baseball hopin' that no one crashed the house windows

'cause nobody mama was payin' for nothin'
'nd ass whoopings could come any which way   like coupons

but that ain't stop us.   nothin' ever really did.

cause 600 banks drive was no curfew
it was boxin' glove throw downs 'nd super soaker shoot outs

jumpin' off of rooftops 'nd icy lady luaus

booty tag 'nd playin' house put our hearts in touch with feelin's hard to
        break free from

mama never really talked to us bout these feelin's.

'nd when we wanted more of our day then sidewalks 'nd nosy neighbors
we combed through spider webs 'nd climbed through holes in wooden fences
to walk the train tracks towards point pinole park.

up on the tracks was a danger that felt like freedom.

knowin' that amtrak would shoot through at any moment,
it was worth the risk to see the bright sky shimmer across the bay

when the train wailed towards us, we scurried to the side
'nd gathered the red rocks to throw at the trains

we loved to see the rocks ricochet back towards us.
a danger that felt like freedom

600 banks drive was no curfew

though by time the sun set our days were well spent

mama didn't always know what we were doin', but we always smelt like outside.

Rodney

(the last time i saw you for the first time in awhile)

the moon was pink
as the day fell sleep
'nd the night curled
in our skin.

on the corners of streets
where i turn mid creep
for an hour, i, 15 again.

behind the yard gate where you stood
towerin' over the fence

you watched me park, bounce out 'nd peel through the gate

to find you 'nd all of our history in a hug

wide
shoulders bulgin'
through black hoodie at the
collar shined a gold medallion;

you smiled diamond teeth

       obsidian skin   with a hustlers hand
               thumbin' blue strips
recallin' the months stretched between us.

you made sales
                    as i *sell* self

publishin'.   you made profit
as i spoke of prophecy.

between your
eyes
'nd my words
your laughs 'nd my ears

the night cold whisperin'
as cars passed
'nd our eyes   followed
hands on guns
behind this steel
gate

you peepin'   me prayin'

i was 15 again.

Troublesome

but only god can judge me — Tupac

it was
a troublesome
'96 that brought us
lil homies so many tears

i remember a bunch of us
young niggaz outside of 600 banks drive

summer shirtless in our skins glory.
crowded on the sidewalk

low posed, crouched foldin' into each other for a picture

while cheesin' 'nd twistin' fingers to w's

with sweaty double knotted soldier rags 'nd sagged pants
bearin' arms flexed up for a kodak

we wasn't there in vegas, but we heard.

we listened from our mothers' radios
days before about the open fire
that struck you on that black starry night.

the details of the story
made me picture you
rollin'
one last time while
breathin', with loomin'
death
around the corner.

i can't c me
as i was
then

but
i know
my dear mama
saw me just like daddy;

gentle 'nd krazy
with a thug's passion
for finger flippin' 'nd
kickin' against
all
odds
in a white
man'z world

'nd
lord knows
it ain't easy for us young
black males when shorty wanna
be a thug 'nd mama's just a little girl.

'nd no, i didn't know you

but it was california's love
that hailed you
as 1
of 2
of
america's
most
wanted
in the
hearts
of
men

DONTÉ CLARK

who felt just as trapped
'nd outlaw'd in somethin' wicked as you.

who run tha streets to the beat
of papa'z song as you,

who's with nothin' to lose 'nd bruised
by the ambitionz az a ridah as you

while tradin' war stories
like somethin' to die 4.

who's young military minded for street fame

peep game from the last wordz
in the ballad of a dead soldja

encouraged to go all out 'nd let em have it
for everythin' they owe me.

though this life i lead
will never be peace.

will never be a fair xchange
for better dayz

cause they don't give a fuck about us
on my block.

'nd no, even if i'm still ballin'
i know this ain't livin'.

though i am told to be
ready 4 whatever

i know all of what shatters when thugs cry.

'nd when you're runnin' on e
in the longest seconds
of last thoughts
thinkin'
about the fullness
of bein' invited into a thug's mansion

beyond here, pauses me

'nd i wonder,
if heaven got a ghetto?

DONTÉ CLARK

Unaware of Harvest

they kill
the children
of israel

on every
corner
in every
crack 'nd
crevice
of american
streets

who are
brothers
of their
bone

'nd piece
of their peace

who make
a boast in
their hearts
at the flowin'
tears of the widow

they care not
that a prince has fallen

nor that a child is mostly skin 'nd ribs

'nd no, they do not consider the rot in their souls

but they
do rejoice in the
swiftness of the sword

plowin' at the neck of
His anointed

while settin' their eyes on the goods of their neighbors

where danger stands 'nd kicks against the land of the
unincorporated

who are not ashamed at their sisters' nakedness
bare babies stiletto steppin' on the blade
makin' merchandise of her fountain

who
at all times
make light
of defilin'
the holy
sanctuary
with their
feast; temples
of the body
with
the abominable
meats on the
breaths 'nd
the blood of
beast in their
teeth

as
they make their hearts
merry on *HIS* sabbath day[s]

unaware of the harvest that draws near.

DONTÉ CLARK

JJ

he was
6'2 mold
of slim muscle
head of hair
wild 'nd thick
as tumble
weeds
loosely
pulled
back into
a braid
'nd wore his
age like
40 years
of guerrilla
warfare

he stares
eyes
familiar with
explosives

he stood
on the
corner 'nd
saw me
comin'
a tip toed
speed
to the tune
of my thoughts
while he
shoulder slanted
a pillar of steal

snarlin' at
the passin' cars
on 23rd 'nd maine

i approached gentle like.

if i could assume
i'd say most times
his mood was like
holdin' a hand grenade

'nd no safety pin
with patience thin as strike lever

'nd richmond streets was
a land of landmines

said he could smell the gunpowder
within me. that i was a hollow point
lookin' to flash 'nd expand on suckas

then he say *you a solid lil nigga*
but ain't nothin' in these streets for you

we done all there is to see out here

keep doin' you, you might be
the one that saves lives

that's when the trigger of me
yielded to ceasefire.

r.i.p. jj

DONTÉ CLARK

Chuk

i was
with you
in your red cadillac
newly bought
20 mins
before
you parked
on 5th
'nd chesley
waitin outside
the liquor
store
for your
pops to
come

before
the car
passed
by
reversed
'nd aimed
12 bullets into
your car

before hittin' you 5 times
'nd dodgin' 7

before the 4 bullets were removed
from your back 'nd thigh with 1
still fragment 'nd cold
lodged in your leg

keepin' that day forever a part of you.

i watched you limp 'nd patch yourself back together

but not fully whole again.

you lived in the bed next to me.

i watched your nights of cold sweats

picturin' the shots discharged
at every sound shakin' you out of your skin 'nd sheets

with all of the guilt chippin' at the corner of me

should i have turned
richmond into a cloud of smoke, for you?

is it selfish 12 years later
to feel like

those bullets should have kissed me.

DONTÉ CLARK

Closed Caskets

cryin' cyphers

circlin' cigarettes, cookies, chain-smokin'
confederate chest coughs couplin' cancers
chiefly chewin' chocolate crowds confidence

cougar countenance
creepin'. cacklin' curses

childish cat callin' caged chained children

can't cease celebratin' crazy crackers currency…

cripples
ca-coon cesspool
crazy … crackers… crackers crackers
crackers created criminals
cool   coo coo celebrity cartoon's
character consumed craniums
contained cargo congo chimpanzees
cuh-cuh-cuzzzz-circus-clowns-cir-cu-late
craazy cheeessee

call circumstances
candor. canons candid
certainly can't cope calm, cancel
collectin' clouds
can campin' crampin'

circumvent contra costa county's
cement cemeteries

change centuries
click click click

calibers chasin'
catchin' chest cavities   *click click*

crossfire   choke   chokin'

closed caskets.

DONTÉ CLARK

KOO DADDY

Their Hearts

shall melt 'nd
their knees
be a puddle
of
water
beneath them
because
their eyes
were
lust
for
grave
danger
'nd their
bones
were
dry of
pr**aisé**

The P's

poor people penny pinchin'
'nd panhandlin' prayers for per diems

prefer pushin' 'nd peddlin'
prostitutin' to participate in purchasin' the presence of presents to
    passtime.

a pathological pathway of the proud

from peasant to pedestal

it's the pain of people

who pretentiously post photos of prized possessions;
paper, pendants, porsches, 'nd pistols

the perpetual penury of particular parentin'
that preludes the p poppin' 'nd parkin' lot pimpin'

a plethora of porches from parchester to philadelphia   patron pourin'
paradin' poison to preteens while police patrollin'

these project parties are a paradigm of pagan pandemoniums

posed as positive
pretendin' pretty preach prolific but be petty

proclaimin' peace with no prosperity

protest protest protest…'til popped by projectile. pause.   then protest.

must be the prey of politics, performers of propaganda
pupils of predictive programmin'

'nd pages 'nd pages 'nd pages of paragraphs

papers by poets 'nd professors philosophyin' 'nd pleadin'
against mass promotion of the piercin' parables of our poverty

pain for profits? hmm, perhaps.   anyhow

—just my personal perspective from *the p's*

Koo Daddy

the toof'less man
stood outside the car door
of the driver side to my father's benz.

before he could sneak into the car
'nd grab us, i rolled all four windows shut
'nd hurried to lock all doors.

daddy was in the back of the strange blue house
where he would always go for hours 'nd could never hear us scream.

the toof'less man leaned onto the car door
searchin' the back seat with his yellow eyes
tappin' his thick crusty fingers against the window.

when he spotted my sister hidin' behind clothes between the seats
    he smiled.

he always came for my sister.

i turned the car key
to power the window down but
not low enough for a fly to creep in. he
pretended to stick his fingernails through the cracked window
as i yelled, *com'on 'nd do it, i bet that stinky thang comin' right off.*

where is she the toof'less man asked, *she can't hide from me.*

get away from my sister, i forced out of my lips through the cracked window.

when he sees my little sister shawny again peekin' from beneath the
    backseat
he grinned wide with his bare gums showin' snappin' his calloused hands
    together

bobbin' his head as his eyes close shut, 'nd sang

cutie pie cutie pie you're the reason why
cutie pie cutie pie you're the reason why

i yell with all of my little body, *get away from my sister punk!*
he rotated his shoulders back 'nd forth snappin' his fingers
his head tilted back as he sang louder

you're the girl that makes me feel so good cutie pie!

shawny hid from the man each time we saw him comin'
as i would poke out my chest motionin' with a threatenin' punch

but

we, shawny 'nd i, both enjoyed how the toof'less man
loved to sing *cutie pie* to my lil sister. he always sang this song, these words
    to my sister.

Granny Mo', Big Worm

i don't know what possessed monkey to do it
what could have formed this small rebellion in her stomach
'nd urged it to crawl with anxious fingers to the back of her throat
stretched her tongue like slingshot loaded with words too heavy
for 6-year-old lips to fling across mama mo's livin' room
to ricochet hallway paint, landin' the burn into granny's skin
but i saw it happen.

it was on a regular sunny day visit up there in montalvin
when my baby sister shawny, soft as puddin', esteemed
with neatly greased pigtails 'nd knocker balls, decided that this day
for whatever reason was the battle ground anticipated to test her
    sharpened voice.
to pull it out with a sassy grip 'nd ebony swing brave enough to cut the
    corners
of granny's couch, slicin' across dinin' room furniture plastic covered
bouncin' against decorated walls framed with older faces
that was young before us, in a fussin' match with our daddy's mama in her
    house.
granny's house.

all of what was said escapes me. not sure what pulled this blade
from monkey's teeth to slice down the full sized woman that
    grandmother'd half
of narf richmond who stared the fright into uniforms 'nd police badges,
    'nd rough necks
but my sister, monkey, was spunky this day.

words flung back 'nd forth, from pebbles to stones between granny 'nd
    monkey
granny 'nd monkey 'nd then
at that moment is when i heard the blade. monkey perched up with all of
    her body,
'nd threw out, *that's why you look like big worm.*

the heart of me fell out of my bowels onto the carpet,
rolled underneath the couch 'nd trembled.
it was the heavy gust of wind that turned the hallway corner,
with flames spinnin' behind the thick glasses framed on granny,
heavy as oak tree, stern as brick in night gown
rushed toward the voice that bled her ego.

monkey, fast as blink of an eye was out of granny's reach,
through screen door 'nd into daddy's car
doors locked before i knew she left. derrick 'nd i
covered with laughter 'nd tears at the thought of
granny likened to big worm off *friday*. the hair rollers in granny's hair was
    the haymaker.

monkey knew if she barricaded herself in the car, she was safe.
but uncle ned was like a nail in a tire. he impressed
upon our ears the bounty for monkey's return
that enticed our eyes with fortune of 5 dollars each;
if derrick 'nd i lured shanwy back into the snare
of granny's leather belt lurkin' in the hallway. in the 90's, 5 dollars
got you anythin' small hands could carry from corner store
enough to trade our sister for sweet tooth fix.

we waited for the heat to beat against the leather seats
in daddy's car. knowin' that monkey would eventually forget
about the sharp edge she slung at granny's heart, 5 dollars would get her
to climb over her fear back into the house…we approached,

uncle ned gave us 5 dollars, 'nd said you gotta come get yours if you want it.
brief hesitation, she bit the bait.

tip toein' through threshold wide eyed at every turn 'nd step,
monkey floated her way to the backroom with uncle ned.
reachin' for her 5 dollars. uncle ned, just as childish as us,
hurled out unto the hallway ceilin', *get the belt*

realizin' the the hallway shrinkin', 'nd space between granny 'nd front door
    closin' in
monkey tried to leap for it. in mid swing, a joltin' thrust, thick leather strap
wrapped around the tail end of my sister,
with a fleshly grip on the slither of monkey's arm
catchin' her in the arm simultaneously.

in that moment, as i jumped through screen door into the blazin' heat
feelin' the sting of monkey's whips 'nd her cries grabbin' at the hairs of my
    back.

it hurt me to see her grieve, but when we all hit the store later eve
oh my, oh my were we well pleased.

Uncle Ned

paralyzed from the neck down

because your best friend
wanted to shoot you into a casket

rob you for stacks of street paper

to ease his jealous heart with your blood
'nd you ain't die easy.

could've had your best friend killed

told your baby brother, my dad,
not to shoot. told all of your people
                    to bring him to you 'nd close the door.

i wonder what words became the healing flesh?
what cloth does one have to be cut from
                    to know that stitches come with it?

behind those walls, was a shooter's tears
'nd your forgiveness that spared his life.

why?

even though the rest of yours would remain
still 'nd limp wadin' on a mattress, or
propped up in a wheelchair

hands curled into socks
sippin' through straws 'nd pissin' in a tube
needing your baby brother to clean you 'nd change your clothes.

                    i still wish that i had went to see your casket
                    it's just was hard to know that you were in it.

r.i.p. uncle ned

My 21st

part 1.

3 days before my 21st birthday

i was called up to the hospital.

my granny *mo'* body was tired
'nd any day soon she would leave here.

i was preparin' to take flight from the bay area
to florida on a boat cruise to bahamas.

a 10 day trip on the island blue
should do my mind some peace.

but granny... my father's mother was tired.
'nd any day soon she would leave here

tubed up 'nd coma like 'nd all
of her heavy was reclined back.

my cousins outside in the waitin' chairs
talked about how granny was earlier that day

she smiled, joked 'nd crazy talked like she do.
her regular.

though i wasn't sure if she would recognize her son's
face on me. so i stood there at the foot

edge of her hospital bed, peelin' back
all of the times granny allowed us cousins stay in her house.

the rabbits she had in her garden
the big fresh carrots i pulled from the soil

the animated bites i gave in her kitchen
self-esteemed as black boy bugs bunny

who was quiet, who smiled mostly 'nd
loved to jump on granny's bed.

that was then, 'nd any day soon
granny mo' might leave here. so i approached

curled my fingers into hers while she slept.
palmed her rough touch. held her heavy.

minutes more into peelin' my memory
she awake, jerk her hand from mines 'nd

don't recognize her son's face on me.
granny was startled. i'm not sure if i scared her

or she'd rather see other faces than mine.
unsure, i stopped back. stepped over the pieces

of me that spilled onto the room floor 'nd left.
i went back to work. floatin' through the blur.

either that night or next mornin', granny mo'
left her body, 'nd any day soon i could too.

r.i.p. granny mo'

DONTÉ CLARK

part 2.

it's like stayin' up all night to stare into the wide darkness
at the back of the ship docked on the shore in the bahamas.

can't tell the sky from the sea. but you hear the waves dancin'
'nd the wind wavin' through before the great star is fixin' to exit

his bedchambers 'nd dart the heavens
raisin' the darkness with a burnt orange to yellow 'nd

you feel the tears. you see your 21st year on an island
'nd you smilin' like, nigga we made it. but granny didn't

'nd most of richmond but right now
that ain't your business. you're not rememberin'

no, for the next 7 days
you're just livin'. just
livin'.

part 3.

i'm at an airport in florida
'nd i receive a call from lil erv

this is the day of my granny mo's
burial 'nd i wasn't gon' make it.

that's why erv was callin' me.

he was anxious to see me at the funeral
but i wasn't there. i was comin' back from the bahama's sands
'nd blue waters while my family was in mournin'.

my cousin sighs.

aight cuz, hit me when you touch down

days later, back in the rich, i call erv 'nd shoot to the hood.
we posted up for hours. from his house we walked

to 5th street corner store. no reason. just to be outside.

while standin' on the corner i told him 'bout the bahamas.
he wanted to hear all about life 'nd the taste of air outside
of narf richmond.

curiously listenin', he was all smiles 'nd banter.

cause see, lil erv had a way about him that richmond loved.
humble with a valor cadence he walked like everywhere was home

my cousin, he had a smile
that couldn't help but leap on to you.

DONTÉ CLARK

'nd no matter how blue you felt, or smoked grey you walked
when lil erv laughed, it was like his way of helpin' you pick up your pieces.

we walked toward the p's....between my eyes is the familiar
lean of gates 'nd homes like seen in nassau. nassau looked like narf.

between my explanation of poetry 'nd life on the road
i enquired about the bullets.

*yo cuz, is it cool for us to be walkin' round here? ain't
been no shootin's lately?*

'nd as cool 'nd unbothered as he be, said, *nah, it's been quiet
out here. like a shootin' every blue moon or somethin'...we good cuz.*

walked 8 blocks down to the p's. posted under the spotlight in the parkin' lot.
we laughed loud, whispered about niggas tellin', 'nd thought about blue waters.

night came 'nd i was headed out.

thanks for comin' to fuck with me cuz.....aye man hit me.

slap five 'nd a shoulder bump. both of us feelin'
full from our banter 'nd brotherhood.

erv tells me to call him. to come back to the hood 'nd see him.

i said i would. but my heart told me not too soon.

it didn't want me flirtin' with the idea of huggin' corners too much.

though i wrestled with my mind to call him, to go back.
i said this for 12 days.

then erv was walkin' home one night 'nd
was shot multiple times. i guess the moon was blue that night.

i imagine his humble spirit in shakes 'nd trembles
his valor cadence in blood 'nd tears

the night bein' the longest winter ever.

'nd our childhood corner holdin' onto his final moments
as he died right there. to be later mourned at 21.

the first homicide of 2011 in richmond. lil erv.

i knew i wouldn't see him for a while, but not like this.
i should've called him. wore his laugh on me again.

i wonder if part of me knew that any day soon he would leave here
or if any day soon it could've been me.

r.i.p. lil erv

DONTÉ CLARK

My Sister, Monkey

is comely as summer nights.

behind her fire
there is a warmth that seeps into you

could hold you gentle
in dark hours

pullin' your eyes to search her thoughts like constellations

mind be bold 'nd wide as black as me

'nd now i love it.

but then as youngin's
from the scars of me i teased her

for bein' a post that the sun had stopped to lean on before settin'

for bein' born with hair that fought back

would curl under water like fist

'nd chip the teeth of cheap combs until bent by brushes
'nd mama's heavy hands

extendin' her curls to waves, neatly in four parts

an arrayed bouquet of flower barrettes

skin smooth as baby-
oil shine

'nd now i see you heavenly

though decades later
i am still haunted by the voice
from the grave i held you over.

Convalescent Home

i sit 'nd listen to the air that circulates the room from the fan right above me.
how the hum of the wind twists 'nd dances around the beeps to the machine
that pressures up 'nd down on the right side of the bed.

i am here at the convalescent home for the third time this week
to visit my paw paw in his old age, after life has requested a leg from him.

the tv plays the national geographic in hushed tone.
between my breaths 'nd long blinks, i see flashes of the blue sea 'nd jungle trees.

i hear a lady in a wheelchair. brown skin. short grey hair.
scootin' through the hallway with a blanket on her lap yellin' *help me.*
no one on staff seems to respond.

my grandfather is lyin' in his bed, with a brown food tray in front of him
'nd a straw comin' out of a styrofoam cup.

his eyes droop.
his voice is a raspy whisper.

he says he's not much hungry. more of a slow head shake when i offer
　　to feed him.

basically i come to see him breathe. to watch the pulse on the side of
　　his neck beat.
yellow eyes blink with a glassy gaze into some future thoughts. or past.
i'm not sure. but for now he breathes.

outside of grandpa's room i see others attempt to escape their boredom 'nd
　　roam the hallways
each cane or wheelchair that passes by carries stories of fragile bones.

grey beards 'nd bald heads.

crooked steps 'nd slippin' hips.

DONTÉ CLARK

pink blanket
green curtain flowin' around the corner of his bed
i peak through to see my grandpa slouched forward.

long arms of brittle bones 'nd wrinkly skin stretched across where his legs
    are no longer.

he moans a half sleep. his hair is shaved down to the specks of grey

while faintly breathin' through tubes in his nose.

his eyes are burnin' out. like he's starin' into the grave or some of his early
    years, perhaps.

he doesn't talk. joke. or even look me in the eyes anymore. he wobbles from
    his waist
to keep his ribs 'nd head up 'nd balanced. noddin' forth 'nd jerkin' back into
    consciousness.

i sit on the edge of the bed 'nd take in his breaths moans.
watchin' the wheelchairs pass by. walkers stumblin' through.

people sittin' in the hallway frownin' at the life that passes them by.

my ears are pulled back into the room at the tv. there's news about evictions
    in san jose.
congested traffic in san francisco due to construction. 'nd updates on the
    warriors 'nd lakers.

i get up to retrieve some ice cold water for my pawpaw.
I bring the white styrofoam cup with the straw close to his lips. he sips 'nd
    sips. slow breathin' then a sigh of relief.

is it good? he replies with, *hell yea*
for another hour or so i sit 'nd wander back to the times that we took for
    granted.
recallin' the songs he'd sing that dreamed out of his acoustic guitar

the openin' of presents 'nd construction of racetracks for hot wheels in
    pawpaw's room

'nd the fact that pawpaw 'nd granny had separate rooms in the same house
    all of my life
was always strange 'nd funny.

'nd now i wonder
where are the families of these elders?
who comes to see them?
does anyone care?
how many of their surgeries are from the food we eat?
the drugs we take? the sufferin' wait for bitter end because of the prayers we
    never sent?

is this the end for us all in old age?
how could i have been a better grandson?

r.i.p paw paw rob

DONTÉ CLARK

My Sister, Monkey, Said

me:

    hey twin. serious question. you don't have to answer right now,
    but i want to know: how does it make you feel when i call you monkey?

monkey:

    hey, lol, i'm okay w/ it. it's the nickname momma gave me (monkey
    doodles) then missy 'nd dad side of the family adopted it.
    now if a stranger call me monkey imma knock the sound box
    out their throat.

me:

    ok. it just was on my mind 'nd i wanted to check.

monkey:

    i appreciate you askin'.
    i know it's not said in a harmful way. dad side literally don't even know
    my name but monkey so i'm use to it
    but ain't nobody off no streets callin' me that.
    lol issa no.

me:

    yea i feel you.

Koo Daddy Continued

before he could finish laughin' at my flimsy attempt
of arm flexin' in my 8 year old strength

another man approached with a limpin' two step stride 'nd stopped next to
the toof'less man. this man's name is dexter.

dexter 'nd the toof'less man were my dad's friends.

both had skin that wore tired 'nd shined dark brown
as if they emerged from the ashes of charred dreams

i rolled the back window down some
then dexter asked, *aye, where Koo Daddy at?*

that ain't his name, i said.
the toof'less man all gums 'nd dexter a chuckle before respondin'

well that's what i callem…now what?

grillin' dexter through the window, as tough as i could sound out my side lip
ioncare what you callem…that ain't his name.

dexter almost ignored what i said to ask the toof'less man
if my daddy was in the house. *wait til i tell Koo Daddy on you… out here cuttin' up.*

so, i'll tellem myself. dexter shrugged me off 'nd turns to leave.

why do you call him Koo Daddy anyway?

dexter limpin' up the driveway in a two-step stride
stop with a mid turn back towards the car 'nd as smooth as he can sound says

cause he Kooo 'nd he yooo Dadddaay

for a long time, i laughed real tears.

DONTÉ CLARK

What Eye Do You See Me With?

i'm askin' because i only brought 2 faces
with me 'nd i want to put on my best   self.

for you. for us. for this hand on gun conversation that's
september to august past due
'nd has burden my back

'nd thump against my dreams.
turnin' my sleep to tears
in this back seat malibu
beneath stars under a
richmond highway
when this ain't all mines to carry in
nights shivers
homeless   so.. i'd

like to know

with what ear did you hear me speak?
cause it's crazy how i say all of that hurt
in the wind between us 'nd i can hear autumn fallin',
the branches witherin' 'nd rivers chippin' away at rock 'nd
doves cryin'.   but chu' though

the tender eye you say you had
now see me sideways   lump'd lifeless somewhere
'nd now   that's not cho' concern 'nd i'm tryna
figure out what
memories i suffer to speak, do you take
as a pile of rocks i lift to bury you in

why does your heart send its lips to kill me?

why do you confuse my questions
as a chisel to the ice your heart-
beat within

what pathway from here
will your feet
take?

DONTÉ CLARK

Prophecy

we've hasted through fires that the south sent after our feet

unintentionally carried the flames of mississippi burnin' with us

on our exodus trail of tears up north   'nd westbound
covered in the ash of jim crow

with the smudge of smoke seepin' into our lungs

crawlin' through our veins

'nd hardenin' its thick coat onto our blood

our children, birthed with a mark that's profitable for persecution

the *bible* speaks of this prophecy

Koo Daddy Before Koo

born in '59
the offspring of a tennessee waltz 'nd ashy knuckles

there was a summer day that brought forth a boy
benevolent black 'nd bloomin' with a silky spirit medley of fire 'nd rain.

on the collar bone of the 60s

i could imagine the mind of Koo Daddy then as child

just a boy growin' into whirlwind 'nd mud floods
of narf richmond under segregated skies

chasin' sidewalks to catch the dreams escapin' his bones

primin' his gentle to

the rasp of coal, while hidin' the depths of his sapphire blue

to be hailed in the streets of narf richmond as the poet of secrets.

DONTÉ CLARK

Like Lively Seeds

planted in the blackest of soils

when faced with the darkest of times

that stretch forth a season

we too must submit ourselves

to the process of provin' ground

to submerge in the matter

'nd break open.

it's in the peelin' out of our shy layers
that we extend our reach

to pull from the deep 'nd
feed from the *richness* of our roots

that has already absorbed the salvation

of rainy days......that's sipped on the early
dew in the holy breeze

'nd grabbed onto the warm smiles
of summer skies

it's in the burial, trial 'nd resurrectin'
anew do we stem to branch off 'nd bear fruit.

what we are is the nature of things

who we are is what we give

to water, one must be a livin' spring

to shine, one must be burstin' with light

to strengthen, one must tear down the inward parts
'nd taste the sweat

of movin' mountains, breakin' chains
'nd untyin' dead habits from the heart

with fattenin' the bones   with myrrh.

it's to stir up in prayer
or be a liftin' voice like trumpet

that gathers the wind
into a sweet breath   ticklin' the leaves

'nd coils of our precious crowns

durin' the graceful footsteps at noon

'nd the lively sway at sunset.

we know that togetherness is how we thrive

our lively seeds, is how we flourish.

Koo Daddy Becomin' Koo

since '68 summer nights
there's been a fright look over your shoulder   that appears to be
prayin' for another day to *run*
while livin' in the life of footsteps in the dark

tells of tales that keep tailin' me through margins of poverty's parables
periled you to the hunger pains of ghetto child

lost 'nd lookin' out the window of a broken home

with no axe to grind in a mean ole world that left you spoiled
slowly trekkin' towards freedom further on up the road

housed to forever sufferin' through the vampin' shadows of underground

how slick to maneuver the sewers of back stabbers
as steady as you were with a solid rock

posted at the end of a junkie chase
for the fire 'nd smoke taste it takes for flyin' high

as they twitch'd 'nd clawed at the night
you were searchin' for a miracle

even as the little child runnin' wild
when the world's at peace with bein' shiftless shady jealous type of people
you knew to listen to the clock on the wall as somethin' to believe in

black caesar outline
with the sunshine in leather skin
known to go for your guns   *but*   preferred to cruise
controlled within   a mellow mood
what allure for their eyes to check out your mind

in my time, i knew of Koo Daddy's koo before i ever met superfly

before i understood
the blood sweat creased in your fingertips
'nd the heavy that dragged in your eyes when the night beat at your heart
'nd chased you solemn with the trouble blues

unaware, i only knew you as Koo   Daddy

5'10 of stoic obsidian   built like prison   complex
like arms of cedar wood   chest of ivory

murry's grease sleeked on the dip of wave currents beneath black slanted
      wave cap
beanie fold hold the cigarette

behind the wheel thumbin' through hundred's of hunnid dollar bills
steerin' on highway with your knees while speedin'

back when money was dirty 'nd paid for christmas summer trips 'nd
      school clothes

before i became a prophetic bullet discharged from the chamber of
      spunk's barrel

there is still a child that mourns
behind the cool in midst of the shake, rattle 'nd roll of a fool's paradise

Koo Daddy Bein' Daddy

Koo Daddy emerges from the blue tarp that swings low over the metal gate
    to the back of the blue house.
the sun is beginnin' to surrender its glory to the pacific, while shawny
    'nd i fight with our stomachs.

with a cool stride 'nd heavy plop into the driver seat, a turn of the key
'nd the brown benz roars.

shawny speaks with a mother's tongue, *what took you so long, i'm ready to go*

ya'll hungry? want some mcdonald's or somethin'?

shawny, a burst of hunger 'nd eager forgiveness names choice options for
    her happy meal.

i too am hungry but more so burnin' with a question, *aye daddy, why all yo
friends ain't got no teeth?*

for a long time, he laughs real tears.

QUIET STORM

DONTÉ CLARK

Bringing the Noise

walkin' on my way
to a youth speaks workshop 'nd
he pulled out a gun.

it's 3 of them 'gainst
me on a busy frisco
street 'nd time's tickin'.

should i grab his gun?
if i do, i gotta shoot
smack all 3 of them.

if i walk away
chances are he might shoot me
shoot me til i'm dead.

then for some reason
i turn into the streets 'tween
stopped cars. walk calmly.

he calls me pussy.
they don't shoot. my ego
made me wish i had

but we all survive.
i walked to youth speaks late, with
thoughts 'bout mlk

Jadakiss

the last kiss
didn't bring
u(s) closure.
it only reminded
me of the things
i've been through by
your side when cruisin'
towards somethin' else, a
somewhere kind to sojourners
seekin' refuge in a land built on the
grounds of what if. like what if our hearts
wasn't full of gunplay, leadin' our conversations to verbal shootouts,
turnin' our years into a single blur of a smokin' gun. like what if you keep ya head up,
'nd our *gone too long* isn't what brings you down? though we both know i tried, 'nd i still believe
it's time i see you without a death wish. while i ponder the what if, will you search *why?*

DONTÉ CLARK

Simba

chillin' with my nephew one day,
in a deep conversation about manhood.
nephew say, *uncle, why you got all that hair on your face?*
i'm like, *cause i don't want to have no naked booty face like you.*

nephew, puzzled by my response then retorts,
ain't no naked booty on my face.
you know you look like Simba off the Lion King?

so i'm like, *'nd who do you look like?*

nephew say, *i'm Tony the Tiger (grrr)*

i'm crackin' up, lookin' down at him on the sidewalk, *cause your name Tony?*

nephew lookin' up at me like *duh.*
i notice his attention on my hair.
uncle how many dreads you got?

i think back to an answer i use to know,
man, i'm not sure, not that many though.

nephew not satisfied at all at my answer blurts
out with all of his body, *well you about to find out.*
count em. right now too.

now i'm taken back at his lil force 'nd how
serious his eyes are about knowin' this number of my locs.
so i decide to see what would happen if i told him, *nah bruh i don't feel like it.*

as suspected, he stepped in closer with his right hand raised into a fist,
eyes locked on me and says so comically, *you gon' count em right now or i'm a*
   sock you.

1,2,3.........i have 117 locs nephew.

so nephew stood there waited 'nd looked on while i circled
my head countin' and recountin' my locs just to tell me
now cut em off. and yo mustache too.

i start crackin' up, cause the thought of him punkin' me has gon far enough.
i gather my laugh into a fake serious clenched jaw an' bend
down to his level with squinted eyes and say,
look here lil dude, you either gon' be Simba, who becomes a King
or you can be one of them sissy naked booty face hyenas that Simba beats up...pick a side.

his fist unravels, his eyes widened 'nd he shook his head in disbelief.

almost in a stutter nephew say, *i don't want no naked booty face uncle.*

with his words bein' musically pleasin' to my eyes 'nd a great laugh
tossin' around in my stomach i looked at him twirlin' his fingers
just hopin' that i would relieve him from this image his imaginative eyes
        have rested on,

i say, *good, now get back.*

DONTÉ CLARK

Laying of Hands

for more than an hour of love
i sit relax'd on a beautiful day
with my back to the middle
of this leather chair, awaitin'
the cure 'nd therapy of coco
butter hands
interested in my head.

'nd with a gentle scratch
the soap suds form, 'nd bubble
'nd lather under hot water
seepin' a minty sensation to
the back of my mind

this feels like a private party.

it's that magic of a beautiful surprise
riffin' in the complicated melody of
the knots in my little locs
coilin' below my brows

an abundance of joy
'nd growth
through a worthy rollercoaster
curlin' 'nd twistin'
from bald fade, to locs
the due process of brown skin testimony

feels like good trouble.

all while knowin' *i am not my hair*
yet still i see there's hope
in healin' this part of my life.

2 hours of steady love
'nd we're headed in the right direction.
with gratitude of an acoustic soul
i'm ascendin' on a chocolate high 'nd i see god
just from the simple touch of your hands.

DONTÉ CLARK

My 25th

who would've thought
that 3 sunsets before my 25th
i would be in a theatre seat
at skywalker ranch

premierin' my first movie.

a documentary of a tale told in a play
but a real story of me. romeo of richmond
'nd all of it's *raw talent.*

i mean, who would've thought
that my life would be at a 2015
sunset in february, knockin' at 25
mournin' my breath, again

'nd friends' faces, a flash of life on big screen
somber 'nd alive in one scene
you blink 'nd they're dead by next.

art 'nd life blurred 'nd preserved
in our richmond shakespearean verse.

the bravado of macho
the whispers of mark
the lost in hammy
the shadow in fame
the music of cass

all of erv 'nd
the pinched nerve of dimarea.

hour glasses burstin' on the sidewalks

young clocks whose minute hands 'nd hour
marks had too soon stopped tickin'.

few of us are present for this premier.

3 moons before my 25th, 'nd all of my years
flashed between 90 minutes of film

i'm watching me stand next to a ghost.

the credits role as every eye in the theatre seats floor tears.

silence between the sniffles 'nd the feelin's of everyone proud,
while internally *romeo is bleeding*

Who Is It That Dares Think

my ways haven't been paved before me?
that my name hasn't already been written in the heavens
ordained to be spoken aloud on lips pressed against the cheek
of wind with the soul of me as a seed
housed in the bowels of my father in girded loin of narf richmond,
placed me in the watered vineyard of mama where the hand
of kindness has reached down 'nd fashioned the skin of me
a blue poem comely cloak in likeness to thunderous
ancient days that cover my inward parts upheld
fattening the bones of me with just mercy.
who is it? which one of you dares speak foolishly
esteemin' me higher than i ought to be?

was it i that birthed me?
that gave myself
the breath
of life
to fill my lungs
'nd commanded my heart to
beat?
when born, fed i, myself,
with meat of liquid gold or tucked myself to sleep?
did my strength preserve me in the moments of my youth
when faced with the bite of growlin' perils
of stray bullets,
broken glass, and alligator swamps for babies
like me, like moses? or some florida plantation
do i have the number counted
of the hairs of my head past and present?
or remember each step
i took before gettin' here?

do you credit me for who put the smile in my heart at the shadowy
whim of things joyful hidden to adult eyes blind and forgetful to see. was it me
that added to my stature an inch, or foot
that staged my journey through the age of boyhood?
was it i that saw me turn
into a man? made my tongue speak?
made my words flesh 'nd lively pictures shapin' in the heads
around me when ears perceive a feelin'?
this feelin' i speak of
have i created it?
to bounce within the space
of my chest 'nd to be cupped into the vapors of this breeze
'nd sound its song a voice into your soul? i mean

what do i really control?

DONTÉ CLARK

Wanton Eyes

a walkin' warning
'nd proverb for wanton eyes 'nd haughty looks.

a stiff neck
'nd raise nose that reaches into
the firmaments blue.

crowned by bonnets,
buns, 'nd bundles
head wrapped in self
a-mazement
with hooped earlobes
stud sparkled with nose jewels.
she's a pride worn wide open
a drippin' stride makin'
a tinklin' with her feet
decked in ornaments of prude
gold draped in fine
linen huggin' the roundness of her full moon.

behind her
are howls from the world
nations of wild dogs droolin' at the thought of her grave
a hunger in mouths
who have discovered her secret parts
she, the art of our hearts
now ravished
an uncovered skirt
wrent
to pieces
her curtains
a window
of opportunity
bare, bent 'nd
welted astray.
a supple pathway; sucked dry.

a holy waterfall of honeydew,
to a parched 4 seasons.
yes sad 'nd true.
our fountain
of youth
turned
a stream
of wormwood
swallowed by
a swarm
of sharp teeth.

her nectar sweet
a bile taste. a summer
sun dressed in blood
once girded in virginity
cloaked in pearl
of modesty 'nd highness,
now, a screamin'
lament of ash
'nd sackcloth?

a butterfly bush struck
to a crown of
baldness?
her high looks
plummet
stiff
to earth
mother of our
majesty
a reproach.
her field
black soil fit for royal seed
to a desolate womb.

look at what we've done.

The Fall

can't tell you which head i was thinkin' with
or which gave counsel to my heart
before my eyes went lookin' through the silence between us
hand pickin' the moments silky as cocoon to blanket our naked
secrets   though at some point my inner boy was reachin' out
with 2 open palms wide like mason jars to catch the butterflies
that emerged 'nd danced around

                        the car ceilin' above us
            then landin' on the cheekbone of your blush as my smile stretches
on top of the warmth of breath foggin' the windows just blinks before sunrise.
was it my heart summoned   or was it the lust in my tongue
        that puckered eagerly to suck from your lips until the honey of you
      was swallowed down fulfillin' my empty daubin' the cracks within me.

2/28

the day has come and spilt itself onto us
flirtin’ outside the car door near the sidewalk

what was suppose’ to be a drive home
has rolled over to the soft touch of pillow talk
in the hours we’ve spent smilin’ through hard questions
’nd puppy love answers
you have taken hold of me
behind this wheel of fortune is a turn of events that i feel out of body for
reluctant to part ways, i tell my eyes to blink away it’s temptin’ to fall to sleep

got a 40 min drive home ’nd a show after noon
’nd this high must carry the way

so we held each other soft and familiar
fit together like broken pieces

then in a flash i was beyond speed limit to the freeway

but when traffic is slow, your eyes tell you to blink for a long second
’nd you’d be straight. another blink ’nd you’d be good

then when traffic clears you be back foot to the peddle

cuttin’ through time ’nd two lanes round windy roads
on highway 4 to richmond, you picturin’ home soon

not knowin’ your eyes been closed all while you’re picturin’
’nd your long blinks happened again ’nd feels like coma

’nd it’s the emergency lane turbulence that awakens you
yankin’ the steerin’ wheel ’nd your car now spinnin’ ’nd twirlin’ 2 lanes in
    its rubber

’nd you’re picturin’ the worse   but no cars hit you

no glass split you   ’nd now your eyes ain’t sleepy no more

’nd behind this wheel of fortune is more time to reflect on the fall

DONTÉ CLARK

Queen

i know a queen
who mothers many dreams
who nurtures when she sings
drippin' water honey springs beam
i know a queen deservin' many things
the double tie of hearts into an art
of wedding rings bling
i know a queen who's likened to supreme
whose love is like a vineyard livin' fruit amongst the green glean
of all that's deemed to properly esteem
our union with future from the fusion of our genes seeen
ding ding how could i get this wrong
i'm butter when it's melted at the alter don't be long
i'm fixin' up a home that's fashioned with holy stones
almond wood willow trees may the heavens sing our song
freely may we roam wherever 4 seasons your granny like my nana
know the family love is deeply keep me
in the parts of you that's wounded by your secrets
i wanna be a witness to healin' all of the pieces needed
a bayou jason lyric type groove poetic full of justice
with a smile that's perfume
zoom to waterfalls sunsettin' our livin' room some things i can't discuss
i'll wait til after jumpin' broom swoon
my favorite tune i love the way you bloom luminary from the riches
i enjoy your full moon.

D'evils

nobody seen the hours i spent
on google searches 'nd youtube links
clickin' 'nd scrollin' through every comment
for clues 'nd views into conspiracies

'nd lately i ain't been in the mood for no regular talk

babies swept missin'
'nd teenage kick backs turn to crime scenes

from hotel bedrooms to basement freezers

it look like
traffic stop by a southern cop
left her hangin' by neck in a cell

i'm tryin' to figure out the hell
is goin' on in us?
what glitters in the eye of my people
that we don't see
d'evils.

Prodigal Son

anything that i have ever touched or claimed as mines
has never belonged to me, i just had it at the time.

when i say anything i mean everything, you name it

'nd i swear to let you know that it wasn't mine.
all that i got here is borrowed.

you know sometimes i get excited 'nd get to slappin' my name on things
cause of how it feels to me or the good lookin' it gives me

but the truth is, it aint mine. 'nd i know how your ears are hard to hear with

so i speak to show you this tricky thing about time. see, too much of it
    causes your mind
to forget things. 'nd not enough of it causes your heart to rebel.
'nd with just enough of it, life a put you at the fork of the road
turnin' between ragin' waters 'nd a dancin' blaze.
you could turn around, go this way, that way   or
you could wait.

now only the single eye knows
what controls the waters is also master of the flames.

yea, i done been here a long while
so long that i thought this was my home.

it wasn't til now that i just remembered that i'm a stranger.

just remembered that i had left my home for a journey
'nd i was supposed to be headin' back with some change.

'nd i had got caught up distracted out here in this old small town

passin' through havin' some fun along the way with some live fellas
'nd pretty gals suckin' down spirits 'nd big cookin'.

feelin' our bellies with all the fatness of the fields.

seemed like a good ol' time til i woke up bound in fetters
sizzlin' from the brandin' iron.
everything i done seen after that been hell 'nd high hopes.

they done mixed up the lines between bein' freeborn 'nd slave

been here so long it all looks the same to old eyes.

so with good drinkin' on my blood i move with the walkin' blues
i just keep on walkin' to the next town over
along the way i done learned how to turn my pains into
profits. from nickels to coon pickles.

got pretty good at it too. yessir, just 'bout know every
way there is to turn to in this town over.

there ain't a bottle i ain't sipped 'nd a coin i ain't flipped.

figured it do me well to be the best at makin' a world of fun
out of all my troubles.

'til just now it dawned on me. i done forgot that this ain't my home.
that i done left 'nd found myself in chains. see i didn't i tell ya,

tricky thing about time is, one mind think times are better, the other mind say
could be worse 'nd better ain't too far   just stick it out.

'til right now, it's my right mind is tellin' me
boy take yo ass back home.

Studyin' Don't Solve Sorrows

so supposedly some say that sweet silence 'nd
spiritual scourgin' should starve out the source of our stupidity.

that the scrapin' of sin 'nd savagery
soaked in our skin is somehow the set services of a southern system

sustained as slavers. self said superiors to susceptible servants

said to slave. seed to seed. season to season. shore to shore.
slaves. saved by slave ship.

something' scary, huh?

such a sad story 'nd a surplus of sufferin' for the swarthy.

so

my strongest suggestions to you
students is to stay strapped. i mean

sharp. smart.

stand tall, sturdy
'nd speak seldomly.

sometimes

sacrificin' speech saves
the sheep from suffer of the sickle.

sometimes
separatin'
self
from showoffs
showboatin'
'nd such silliness
may
salvage some
sewaged soul

surrounded by
silhouette
of
sinkin' ships
'nd sharp shooter's
shootin' of 7.62's.

sure, some say it's safe
to slip through the shadows

side steppin' snares 'nd

study. to stay studyin'

yet still, studyin' don't solve sorrows.

'nd

scratchin' surfaces shuckin' 'nd stutterin'
slumped shoulder sounds like straight sucka shit…

i mean stupid.

shuckin' 'nd stoopin'
for stipends 'nd statues are now suspended

so

stand straight

stay solid

if study
then study *scriptures*

seven sunsets straight

seekin' the sure shalom of shiloh.

DONTÉ CLARK

Powered Up

steam spiral
from the wide cup
tilted towards my lips

a small matte black sweatshirt
huggin' my mornin' shivers warm

fast steppin' the sidewalk
side eyein' the squirrel
dartin' 'cross the sunlit pavement

i'm smilin' towards the cat
leaned back in the lawn lickin' its fur

bluebirds an upbeat chirp
praisin' through this autumn sky

blue sketchers on my feet
collectin' 2 miles easy

before sweat glands perspire

my heart dances while my thoughts leap
'nd my spirit a tall cup overflowin'

for a long stretch of moments,
i'll be powered up

BONES REBIRTH

Telephone

thinkin' thoughts trauma teaches
      thinkin' they tryin' to train those of us that's thoroughbred
to talk tersely 'nd timid
                        to teeter
             teeter til teeterin' teaches us to traipse to the third trace of
     toddler. to be trippin' 'nd tumblin' ten thousand times til we're tossed
over to the tango of tauntin' tales that's told to us

bout their tenacious taboos.

the tragic traffic that track-list the torture that's tattooed in the thrustin' trials
trekkin' with tribulations always
        there to twist 'nd touch
the torsos of the talented ten.
                 the targeted.
                         the ten toes
of the toughest teenagers traumatized from the terrible
tactics that the tyrannical task force use to   tame us
by torch. they're temptin' to tear through our time. tuh,

there's too too many teachers that's thievin' the temples
takin' til the temples be tilted tired of tithin'.
this piece be tipped to them to the tongue tied
tired ticks that's trickin' the people to trap 'nd trample triple out their treasures
                             trashed to the totality of
the treacherous terror-domes

the tasteless territories that the thugs tend to. tuh

there be telephones that televise the tirade of toxic tears
that's truism.   the typical thinkin' the thoughts
that trauma teaches the thinkin'.
go through total turmoil just to tell our tribal testimony.

through telephones.

Heads Kept on Swivel

sometimes it's you
not stoppin' at stop signs.

sometimes it's you 'nd the crew ridin'
with the glock 9 on opp time.

sometimes it's highway flyin'
side street slidin'

car still runnin'
clutchin' while gas pumpin'

dippin' dodgin' 'nd high sidin'

music on blast doin' the dash scrapin' pass
sucka duckin' but ain't sparin' nothin' when y'all cross paths

smash.

burnt rubber 'nd broken glass

it's sad but i ain't lyin'

don't hardly know a street in the city
where we ain't dyin'.

yes, at all times
all heads kept on swivel.

DONTÉ CLARK

Blood Drippin'

blood drippin'
blood drippin'
all
over yo sneeaakks

blood drippin'
blood drippin'
hung twisted
under
the leaves

young gifted
so young gifted
wrung drenched
by hands of police

they love trippin'
our blood drippin'
cause slugs spittin'
tearin' our t's

awaken to a call
by one of my dawgs
say he heard somebody
tell
somebody that
that one body
erybody been lookin' for left his body

at the mall...

still in my draws
droopy eye searchin' the walls

i recall a collapsed lung
a gasp break dip jerkin' type of run

blood drippin'
who knew 18 to 21 would be the hurdle
jump that borrowed the meanin' to
we shall overcome... some say

blood drippin'

our love's missin'
bone cripplin' over dem c's

blood drippin'
blood drippin'

they want me to die on my knees

at least dr. king seen 39
back when black men mostly died
by picket lines

oowee ooh my not these times

blood drippin'
blood drippin'
blood drippin'
out in these streeets

jump man be logo for corner store cleats
bear chest black beast runnin' buck 'nd wild in these streeets

blood drippin' over our sneeaaks

overheard words of blak birds

laughin' at the herds.. a laughin' livestock
who lies stocked prison high
ain't you heard?

bluebirds circlin' cornrows 'nd afro's

be'neath devil eye surveillance
chemtrailin' my trail of tears... slave dreamin' all these years
aim high niiigga   reach for your crown
'nd be king already...

hmm not here hope is too heavy 'nd american dreamin'
is deadly

aren't you tired of drippin'   bein'

a cry at sunrise
wailin' terror-dome of skin

bones fried rope tied chin

hung twisted under the leaves

our place of worship
once springin' livin' water
now bitter wormwood

hung twisted under the leaves

underneath she stood
once a womb now sterile grave
birthed kings, buried slaves

kill for the new j's
risk my whole entire life
3 strikes, in their cage

they want me to die on my knees

takin' on their ways won't free us
from our rage... not a page from their book
holds true... except for the parts that they pretend
that they you.... peekaboo
seed of their fruit
tell you who is who. . .
why don't you get a clue
'nd
keep
it
down
deep
deep
down

crowned
in our blood

everlastingly holds heavenly told secrets...

i mean it

blood drippin'
blood drippin'
blood drippin'
i can't breathe

blood drippin'
our loves missin'
i pray the most high relieves

all praises all honor all glory
all ages do honor our story
all praises all honor all glory
anime illustrates our stories.

DONTÉ CLARK

Fist

there was a Fist that took over all corners
of city streets overflowin' the intersections
to downtowns. a Fist that slaved four centuries
to climb the capital ladder. steep'd up chiseled rock
of mount rushmore to reach freedom heights
where eagle is awaitin', baskin'
in the sweetness of apple pie.
around the lips 'nd eyes of time, this Fist,
the hand of it, has already aged. weary 'nd
bruised bein' half wake less dead 'nd slippin' slumber
often into sunken place. slept on 'nd lost feelin'
to numbness til these sudden shakes awaken
its fingers from american dream(in') again. it happens
every ear to the streets moment when hearin'
the bombs explode from the badger's gun,
pausin' the Fist. forced it still 'nd sweaty, overthinkin'
then fumblin' to grab the body that dropped at the nail
of its fingertips. hesitated 'nd unsure of its grip, it feared
to lift the weight of the knee heavy to the back of a neck
surrenderin' a black body's breath to the asphalt

sendin' sizzlin' spirit spiralin' into the ether.
feelin' at fault, 'nd helpless the nerves of the hand
the fist shook 'nd thumped out of its skin with its veins
eruptin' from the boil of its blood. this hand, i mean
Fist, was now up. it was woke again curlin' into itself
its strength a Fist poised 'nd angry that moved
with audacious speed 'nd a dare that humbled
evenin' traffic with historic fear at the might
of its punch. captured between the twitchy eyes
of camera phone drunk in a teary gaze,
the knuckles raised lofty 'nd squeezed
with a chant smokin' from the bone

as if between the creases of the Fist finger bite
ate at the neck of uncle sam luggin' his throat
from the lynch rope on the Fist shoulder
liftin' sam's wrinkled feet above the fire of
dead presidents.

Mirajj

we overcame their nights by fire.

poured 'nto streets with spewin' heat
ignitin' a fallen sky tequila sunset.

because there was nowhere to hide
all souls 'nd soil purged together.

we knew this day would come

we've prayed 'nd waded murky waters
aside bloated babies 'nd charred bones
cravin' the taste of this jubilee.

peaceful protestin' stirred a war cry

holdin' signs while kneelin' down only
gotten us shot, jailed, or vanished.

there was no way around it.
with no justice, peace escapes us.

america, an evil child born rotten
burstin' with a belly of flies

only had a taste for killin'

out of options 'nd nothin' left.
price for our freedom was death.

we overcame their knights by fire.

carried our weight with bleedin' knuckles,
through the flames…seekin' to redeem.

we knew this day would come

leapin' over ashes of mount rushmore
my heart makes noise within me.

heavy sounds pullin' for new tears
to submerge earth a holy baptism.

forsakin' seedless vines of strange fruit
for an endless bite outta heaven.

with parched lips we sit numb.

sun 'nd moon cover their eyes.
untyin' our souls, we mourn. deeply.

our tears walk on the wind.

in prayer, we uplift the dead;
rememberin' each soul precious 'nd unique
as black sand, kissin' the sea.

iron yokes removed, 'nd tables turned
though memories of what happens haunts.

we knew this day would come.

"Mirrajj," previously published in *Black Freedom Beyond Borders: A Futuristic Idea of Abolition Day.* The Wakanda Dream Lab, PolicyLink, and The Big We. August 2020.

DONTÉ CLARK

Pistol Play

drivin' 2 hours south to the countryside of california
beneath the mornin' clouds i'm standin' in the rain 'nd red mud
with a white man at the back of his truck
helpin' him unload his box of pistols 'nd rifles
'nd bullets for a day of shootin' targets.

the metal discharge 'nd fire
projectile through flesh of blue paper.

the gun smoke 'nd wet rocks catch the wind.

i started to record my pistol play

but nah

nobody needs to see that i been out here shootin'.
cause if it ever come a time for me to be shootin'

whoever i'm shootin' at gone know fasho
that i'm pretty good at shootin'.

Pistol Play, Hit Different

after a full day of pistol play 'nd drivin' back to where phones get service
'nd you are alerted to the buzz 'nd vibration of missed messages 'nd voicemails.

you skim through the names as you drive 'nd wonder why so many calls.
you make a mental note to call back later then the calls come ringin' again.

some calls be back to back too many from some names who don't often call
too much anyway. so you answer.

'nd sometimes on this type of call it be your sister
who be callin' to tell you about that thing again.

you know, that thing about somebody killin' somebody else in richmond
'nd have you heard? only this time that somebody else is that somebody
you love who somebody had just killed.

so you cry.

with too much road back home before you

with the type of music that put you in all of the feelings
for not havin' no feelings about killin'

'nd your mind is turnin' like the speedin' tires you speed with

'nd your hands are rememberin' its full day of pistol play

'nd you say to yourself, this song hits different.

DONTÉ CLARK

Red Skies

when i received the call

'nd heard the tale of someone who had chased you down
'nd stood over your body,

that triggers 'nd hammers
flashes 'nd fires were sent

to blaze through your holy temple,

all of me had broken.

the peace that i forgathered 'nd fumbled with

right then had caught match, melted, 'nd spilt
all onto the curb for onlookers to study the mess of me

my eyes, a red sky
widened, thundered 'nd poured heavy

drownin' out the train of sirens 'nd voice of reason.

i could taste your last breath twirlin'
in the spring air above me

but couldn't feel the earth beneath my wobblin' feet
or calm my blood from pacin' around the hollow of me —

it's just that i've known that bitter taste of death before
'nd my palate had grown a cravin' for danger.

i can't say that i prayed.

though my heart then referred to as a godly book

had suddenly been pages torn with bloodstained verses

ripped pieces flutterin' through the night.

long ago, i foresaw that day
comin' sneakin' its way to break 'nd enterin'

hog tie my soul a hostage to grief

to fog my memory of your lambency
to stumble my steps over poems, promises 'nd my preachin'

for reachin' for our king's dreams

'nd hopes to enter our rest into a thug's mansion

so neither of us will be a ballad

bellowed by block boys
before our beloved birthdays

but now

here i am
pickin' up 'nd piecin'
together what shattered

recollectin' pieces of my peace
'nd prayin' away red skies from my eyes.

r.i.p. dimarea

DONTÉ CLARK

Night Shift

you sleep
like wakin' up
is the icin' on the cake

'nd
i awake
like sleepin' is only
somethin' i could daydream

insomnia

Soul Cravings

the holes
within me
are seekin'
to fill
themselves
with
the salts,
the sugars,
'nd the lips
of the world

DONTÉ CLARK

Shabbat

it's the song
that's soft
sittin'
on
the
breath
of
little
prayers

fillin'
pages
of a
blues
book

stored
on
the shelf
in the heart
who has labored
for heaven 'nd
earth to meet

it's 6 days scurryin' to the 7th, to set yourselves in place at dusk.
to be, not hands 'nd feet, but a reclined back 'nd sealed eyes.

a hum repeated at the arch of sun

at the flippin' of your heart like the turnin' of soil

receivin' the psalms as the plantin' of righteous seed
to be the blade of herb that reaches

at the ease of brows 'nd the pleasurable sips of lemon squeezes

rest in the bosom of shabbat

behold joy between the feet 'nd fingernails in dirt

thankful to soon reap what you've sowed in its comin' season.

savor your bitter with sweet without ceasin'

step by
step by
'nd bye

DONTÉ CLARK

The Sky is Fallin' 'nd my Hands are Full

there are emails to be sent, with signature'd contracts 'nd signed w-9's

pictures to be taken 'nd posted 'nd liked 'nd shared

cars to be sought, 'nd bought, 'nd flossed

'nd a body thick in parts that needs to be trimmed 'nd slimmed gym'd
for summer swims

cause i hear there are soft sands 'nd beaches everywhere that i should be in
touch with for sure

but the news today says that the sky is fallin', 'nd my hands are full

'nd beyonce just dropped another 1, 'nd i'm here for it

'nd verzuz is live in 20 mins

'nd tyler perry's new show premieres tonight 'nd i'm drunk 'nd still drinkin'

'nd football, 'nd football, 'nd football….'nd what? turn that up

oh snaps, the homies just pulled up 'nd it's lit 'nd we lit 'nd we all
with the shits

'nd through our red eyes 'nd window tents we in search for all the smoke

'nd whatever blunt, barrel or cell it comes with

cause they keep talkin' bout the sky is fallin'   'nd my hands are full 'nd ain't no worry to be had here, no concern or care for to be counted

'cause quarantine mask 'nd washed hands is the plan

6ft of separation heals a nation til vaccines get us cleaned

cause coronavirus ain't linked to no coronation nah, hell nah

crown for who? for us? black people? hell nah. sounds of conspiracy

'nd i ain't got time for it. the sky is fallin' 'nd my hands are full

                    i catch up with you later

DONTÉ CLARK

Eyes

there was sorrow that consumed the eyes of the livin'

a burnin' ague in the hearts of many

why has the sky
been as iron to us?

why has the land been as needles 'nd thistles to our sides
'nd spikes to our feet?

where is the blessin'
of our Lord?

has his kindness stayed there
on the other side of our middle passage?

Between Worlds

in the lambs'
silence
there is a ghost
who walks in
the tall grass
durin' the
keepin'
hours
'nd
every time
i die
beneath
the
leaves
the legacy
of the bones
rebirth between
worlds

Exodus

the sun came
on summer
as
i greeted
the dawn.

wearin' sword 'nd fury
like fine clothes to the jew
as prophecy that speaks
to a black thunder
'nd *the fire next time.*

i've been urged to come
out of the wilderness
from the shadow 'nd act
of an invisible man
'nd called to weep. noddin' by
de' fire in my two
little boots with
nowhere
to hide
cause
he sees through stone.

with tender heart
this simple speaks his mind
like the *negro speaks of rivers*
of another country
as flesh
'nd bone though
i, too,
am an american
just not
with-
out laughter in some plantation portrait.

        aah
now i see.
our second exodus
has come; like brothers we meet.

his radiant glory
pours into me
a rage
righteous
'nd strong as
black samson 'nd burgundy wine.

by
the right
hand of the most
high, i be the somebody
that blew up america. though it seems like nobody
        knows my name
i'll be sure
to *go*
tell
it
on
the mountain.

DONTÉ CLARK

Today, I

sat across from
a black panther

who spoke
with all of the 60s in detail
as vivid 'nd lively as today was then
with a concert of black fists raised
in the tone of his voice 'nd his eyes
a gaze of sidewalks 'nd state capital steps stormed
with black boots on the stride of bad brothers with soul sistaz grippin'
freedom with fingers on triggers 'nd pointed barrels
at the flag 'nd its evil in its eagle seekin'
to dig its claws 'nd crooked teeth into the scalp of ripened
fruit of buddin' black thoughts

that breathed movement
into the hands that held books,
'nd warmed plates of free breakfast,
'nd newspaper black ink ridden with pigs 'nd righteous
rage in the furrowed brows on party people with a love
for equal that's black... that's black as all
get out with palms open 'nd reachin' reachin' within reachin'
wide reachin' for high almighty 'nd not for dollars
not for pockets not for american pies or seats at white tables but for ours
for land that look like us
before the blood cried out from the roots
'nd metal pillars held our futures behind them or saliva
in the belly of swine hunger at the sirens of pigs snoutin'
our leader's trail to liberty 'nd eatin' it all up

these hands were reachin'
not to steal or loot but to take... yes
to take...
to take back
to take back
back all of its power
'nd purpose
'nd people
'nd programs
'nd prophets
protectin' property proclaimin' power
for all of its people in the name of the party.

today i
sat across from
a real black panther

'nd 30
minutes in
i had become one

DONTÉ CLARK

Blessed Be

all those who fear the strong hand

who are knees to the humble
'nd a face to the dirt

who speak from a rented heart
repented 'nd lamentin' its bones

with lips that are washed with
prayers 'nd psalms of david

seekin' the mercy that
endures forever

blessed be the mercy that ensures forever

blessed be
the mouth of thanksgivin'

for the belly that is pleased
with its daily bread

'nd the eyes that await
the hour of the thief in the night

blessed be the flame to the oil

the loins of the mind
that is girded with faith

'nd the feet that are quickened
to the gospel of peace

blessed be the ears
that are pressed to the sky

rejoicin' at the comin'
down of the promised city

blessed be the waters
of new y'erusalem

30 Peace

when you are no longer countin' the dead more than you are the livin'

'nd when you have learned that being right matters none as much as
   apologizin' 'nd forgivin'

that you are no longer gunpowder but a prayer 'nd frankincense

that your energy is your richness 'nd currency

'nd that time is where you spend it

'nd though the graveyard is pendin' your life's deposits

have no limits. so live it. wisely spend it.

DONTÉ CLARK